COLOURFUL AUSTRALIA
KOALAS

Produced by
Ted Smart & David Gibbon

Featuring the Photography of
Neil Sutherland

Published by Colour Library Books for
GORDON & GOTCH LTD

ARAFURA SEA

TIMOR SEA

INDIAN OCEAN

Torres Strait

DARWIN

Arnhem Land

Cape York Peninsula

GULF OF CARPENTARIA

CORAL SEA

Kimberley Plateau

NORTHERN TERRITORY

Barkly Tableland

Cairns

GREAT BARRIER REEF

Great Sandy Desert

The Granites

Cloncurry   Richmond

Townsville

Macdonnell Ranges

QUEENSLAND

Mackay

Gibson Desert

Alice Springs

GREAT DIVIDING

Rockhampton

WESTERN AUSTRALIA

Ayers Rock   Simpson Desert

Bundaberg

Shark Bay

Great Victoria Desert

Lake Eyre Basin

Charleville

Grey Range

Toowoomba   Ipswich

BRISBA

Lake Eyre

SOUTH AUSTRALIA

RANGE

Geraldton

Kalgoorlie

Nullarbor Plain

Flinders Range

NEW SOUTH WALES

Maitland

PERTH
Fremantle

Broken Hill

Newcastle

Port Pirie

SYDNEY

Elizabeth

ADELAIDE

CANBERRA

Wollongong

Spencer Gulf

VICTORIA

SOUTH AUSTRALIAN BASIN

Ballarat   MELBOURNE
Geelong

TASMAN SEA

Bass Strait

TASMANIA

Launceston

Queenstown

Hobart

The Publishers wish to thank THE LONE PINE SANCTUARY for their kind assistance in the preparation of this book.

Published in Australia by Gordon & Gotch Ltd.

First published in Great Britain 1984 by Colour Library Books Ltd.
© 1984 Illustrations and text: Colour Library Books Ltd.,
Guildford, Surrey, England.
Colour separations by Llovet, Barcelona, Spain.
Printed and bound by Gráficas Estella, Spain.
All rights reserved.

ISBN 0 86283 133 4

TITLES IN THE COLOURFUL AUSTRALIA SERIES

Animals of Australia
Wild Flowers of Australia
Perth
Koalas
Melbourne
Tasmania
Adelaide
Brisbane
Canberra
Sydney
Ayers Rock and the Olgas
The Great Barrier Reef
The Outback

Perhaps more than any other animal the koala symbolises Australian wildlife and Australia itself. It has been the basis of many advertising campaigns concerning Australia, which has only served to enforce the image. The wide-eyed appeal of the creature is irresistible to anyone who sees it and has resulted in the koala becoming the model for many children's toys. This, in turn, is partly responsible for its nickname 'The Australian Teddy-Bear'. The slow-moving vegetarian is a threat to no-one and this, combined with its fluffy ears and 'tennis ball' nose, has given it a charm which ensures it a special place in the hearts and affections of millions.

The koala, along with most other native Australian mammals, belongs to the curious group known as marsupials. The marsupials are an ancient and rather primitive group of mammals, characterised by the presence of a pouch in which the young shelters until it is old enough to fend for itself. In most marsupials the pouch faces forwards, but the koala's pouch faces backwards, making it an unusual member of an unusual group. Even after the young koala has left the pouch it will still cling to its mother's back, where it can stay safe from harm.

The marsupials first evolved some 120 million years ago when the dinosaurs, such as *Triceratops* and *Tyrannosaurus rex*, roamed the earth. In those far off days the world was a very different place, the climate was much warmer and the first birds and flowers were only just beginning to appear. But more important for the story of the marsupials, and so ultimately that of the koala, is the fact that the continents were arranged differently. Australia, South America, Antarctica and Africa were joined together into one large landmass, known today as Gondwanaland. On this landmass flourished the marsupials and, after the extinction of the dinosaurs, they became the dominant group of creatures. Over the millions of years which followed, the continent of Gondwanaland broke up as a result of continental drift. In time the constituent parts of Gondwanaland came into contact with landmasses inhabited by more advanced placental mammals which rapidly pushed the marsupials to extinction, but not in Australia. The island continent and South America remained free from contact with the outside world for about sixty million years. This allowed their fauna to evolve along curious lines, creating many strange and wonderful creatures, including the koala.

For many millions of years the marsupials were free to evolve and adapt in peace and quiet. While they floated on their continent rafts, they evolved into many forms. Some, such as the koala, were unlike anything else, but some developed along similar lines to placental mammals elsewhere. This is a result of convergence, evolving to fill a similar role. South America once had a particular marsupial hunter that developed long, stabbing teeth and was very similar to the sabre-tooth cat. In Australia, there is still a small marsupial, just a few centimetres long, that is so similar to a European mole that it is hard to believe that they are not closely related.

The linking of South America with North America spelled doom for most of the marsupials there, and at one time it was feared civilisation could destroy the Australian marsupials. The destruction of the native habitat, particularly forest and swamp, by white men resulted in a dramatic decline in the numbers of many species. Other marsupials suffered from the competition of introduced species of placental mammal. Placental mammals are, on the whole, rather more intelligent and better adapted than their marsupial counterparts. The marsupial 'wolf', the *Thylacine*, was once prevalent over the whole continent but the introduction of the dingo pushed it from the mainland. The *Thylacine* could not hunt as efficiently and so lost out in the race for survival. Conversely, the brush-tailed possum has increased its numbers dramatically as it moves into an urban environment. The arrival of the white man was almost disastrous for the cuddly koala. The need for building materials and other necessities drove him to fell great areas of forest. This loss of habitat had nearly driven the delightful koala to extinction by the 1920s, but luckily prompt government action saved this charming creature for future generations to enjoy. Indeed, the koala is now staging something of a comeback. An important place for the preservation of this delightful creature is the Lone Pine Koala Sanctuary at Fig Tree Pocket. This centre is open to the public and is an important tourist attraction in Queensland.

The koala itself is, of course, blissfully ignorant of its forbears' ancient history. It is content just to climb around in the branches of the eucalyptus tree munching away at the oily leaves on which it lives. In fact this eighty centimetre long marsupial eats the tough leaves of the eucalyptus tree to the exclusion of all else. In its natural state this was no great problem as there are vast numbers of eucalyptus tree covering much of eastern Australia. In fact it was something of an advantage for the koala became far more efficient at digesting eucalyptus leaves than any other animal and so was able to survive much better. The only thing that the koala must be wary of is being caught on a eucalyptus branch when it falls. An unfortunate side effect of eating eucalyptus leaves is that the small marsupials smell very strongly of eucalyptus oil, which puts many a young admirer off the animal. Otherwise the diet seems ideally suited to the koala as individual animals have been known to live as long as twenty years.

After a history dating back many millions of years, it is good to know that the koala is safe from extinction. Today, the cuddliest marsupial of them all can be found roaming through the eucalyptus forests of Queensland, New South Wales and Victoria. Totally protected from hunting, this appealing creature has an assured future and will, no doubt, continue to charm and enchant generations yet to come.

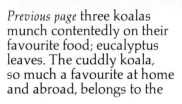

Previous page three koalas munch contentedly on their favourite food; eucalyptus leaves. The cuddly koala, so much a favourite at home and abroad, belongs to the curious order of mammals, *Marsupialia*, members of which are largely confined to Australia and can be identified by their pouches.

The talons of the koala
opposite page make it a
wonderful tree climber
these pages and overleaf

As with all mammals, an albino koala will sometimes be born. They are, however, extremely rare and the only example in captivity is to be found at the Lone Pine Koala Sanctuary at Fig Tree Pocket, Queensland.

Even the sedate koala has its problems; the koala *right* has found a way to get rid of an awkward itch.

The koala is well known for its addiction to the eucalyptus leaf, indeed it will eat nothing else.

Fortunately, the coasts of Queensland, New South Wales and Victoria are thick with eucalyptus trees.

The young koala spends much of its time in its mother's pouch. At the age of about two months the baby may leave the pouch and cling to its mother's stomach, but it is not until about five months that it will adopt the familiar 'piggyback' position.

These pages and overleaf the gentle koala is famous for its ability to nap at odd moments.

The mute, wide-eyed appeal of the koala and its 'tennis ball' nose have endeared it to the world.

Among the more distinctive features of the koala are its fluffy ears and inquiring glance.

There is only one species of koala living in Australia today, the *Phascolarctos cinereus*, but there are several differences between the koalas of the north and those of the south which are generally stronger and have thicker fur.

Koalas make good mothers, the young being carefully protected and fed by the female.

Koalas produce a harsh, discordant cry which is a common sound echoing around the bush.

In common with most other Australian marsupials, koalas have an obscure ancestry, there being a very poor fossil record. However, palaeontologists have found fossils of a related genus, *Perikoala*, which may shed some light on koala evolution.

Koalas are basically
nocturnal creatures, so it
is not at all unusual for
them to spend their days
sleeping or resting among
the eucalyptus branches.

Being a generally inoffensive little creature, it is perfectly safe for humans to handle the appealing koala. Several zoos and parks allow visitors to do just that, the Lone Pine Koala Sanctuary, near Brisbane, being one of the best known. However, the strong smell of eucalyptus oil exuded by koalas has put many people off them for life.

The koala is far more at home in the trees than on the ground, indeed it is distinctly ungainly out of the branches. Unlike most other arboreal marsupials, the koala has a pouch that faces backwards.

In the wild albinos rarely survive because of lack of camouflage, in captivity they are safe and flourish.

Though fairly tame creatures, koalas are not particularly easy animals to keep in captivity. The demands of their diet, which consists exclusively of eucalyptus leaves, cannot be met by the few trees in the koala enclosures and consignments of leaves are brought in from outlying rural areas.

The tough leaves of the eucalyptus are not among the easiest things to digest. The koala has a specially adapted digestive system to cope with them.

It would be difficult to imagine Australia without the cuddly koala, but in the early years of this century disease and the guns of fur trappers reduced their numbers. Legal protection has enabled the koala population to rise again.

Though the koala looks cuddly and is quite inoffensive it is more than capable of inflicting nasty wounds with its claws if it should feel threatened. Wouldbe cuddlers should always be careful.

The small koala can easily munch its way through 1½ kilograms of eucalyptus leaves every day.

The mobile features of the koala allow for a wide variety of expression, from the dormant individual *above* to the wide-awake koala *right*.

CAPE TOWN 10645
SYDNEY 749
WELLINGTON 2513
LONE PINE 20 metres
TOKYO 7148
LONDON 16423
LOS ANGELES 11640
EDINBURGH 16913
HONOLULU 7884
FRANKFURT 16132
AUCKLAND 2297
HONG KONG 6937
KUALA LUMPUR 6482
ROME 15511
ATHENS 14452
PARIS 16254
MOSCOW 13947
SINGAPORE 6153

Young koalas, used to riding on their mother's back, will grip hold of almost anything warm and furry, even a dog, as shown at the Lone Pine Koala Sanctuary *opposite page and top left.*

The curiously appealing appearance of the koala is known the world over and has come to be as representative of Australia as the kangaroo, Ayers Rock and the tough 'digger' image. Its enduring charm should last for many years yet.